SHAKESPEARE

Three Stories by
Charles and Mary Lamb

SHAKESPEARE

Illustrated by
Judy Mastrangelo

Three Stories by Charles and Mary Lamb

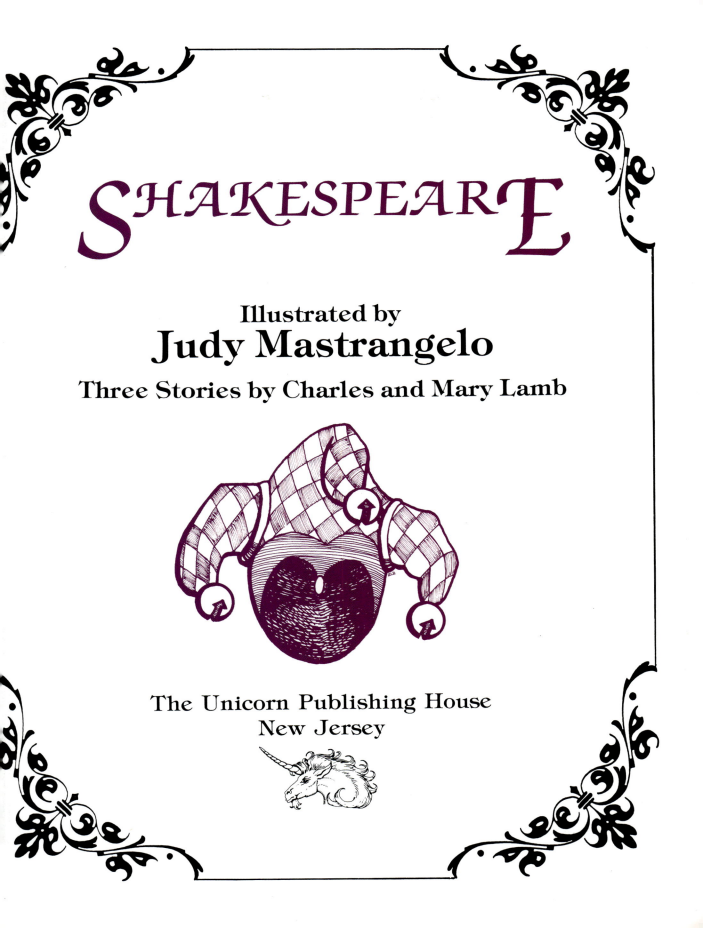

The Unicorn Publishing House
New Jersey

Editor: John Ingram
Art Director: Heidi K.L. Corso
Printed in Singapore by Topan Printing Co., PTE. through Palace Press, San Francisco, CA

Distributed to the book trade in Canada by Doubleday Canada, Ltd., Toronto, ON

Distributed to the toy and gift trade in Canada by Brigitta's Imports, Concord, ON

Special thanks to the entire Unicorn Staff.

Printing History 15 14 13 12 11 10 9 8 7 6 5 4 3 2 1

Library of Congress Cataloging-in-Publication Data
Lamb, Charles, 1775-1834.
[Tales from Shakespeare. Selections]
Shakespeare / illustrated by Judy Mastrangelo.
p. cm.
Summary: A prose retelling of "Romeo and Juliet,"
"A Midsummer Night's Dream," and "The Tempest."
ISBN 0-88101-094-4
1. Shakespeare, William, 1564-1616 — Adaptations.
[1. Shakespeare, William, 1564-1616—Adaptations.] I. Lamb, Mary, 1764-1847. II. Mastrangelo, Judy, 1944 - ill. III. Title.
PR 2877.L3 1989
823'.7 — dc20   89-4918
CIP
AC

Additional Classic and Contemporary Editions
Richly Illustrated in
The Unicorn Heirloom Collection:

ROBIN HOOD
JOURNEY TO THE CENTER OF THE EARTH
GHOSTS: A CLASSIC COLLECTION
PHANTOM OF THE OPERA
AESOP'S FABLES
POLLYANNA
DAVY AND THE GOBLIN
TWENTY THOUSAND LEAGUES UNDER THE
SEAS
PETER PAN
ANTIQUE FAIRY TALES
PINOCCHIO
POE
WIZARD OF OZ
DRACULA
HEIDI
A CHRISTMAS TREASURY
TREASURES OF CHANUKAH

To my
twin brother Jerry,
with fond memories of
our childhood together.

Judy Mastrangelo

CONTENTS

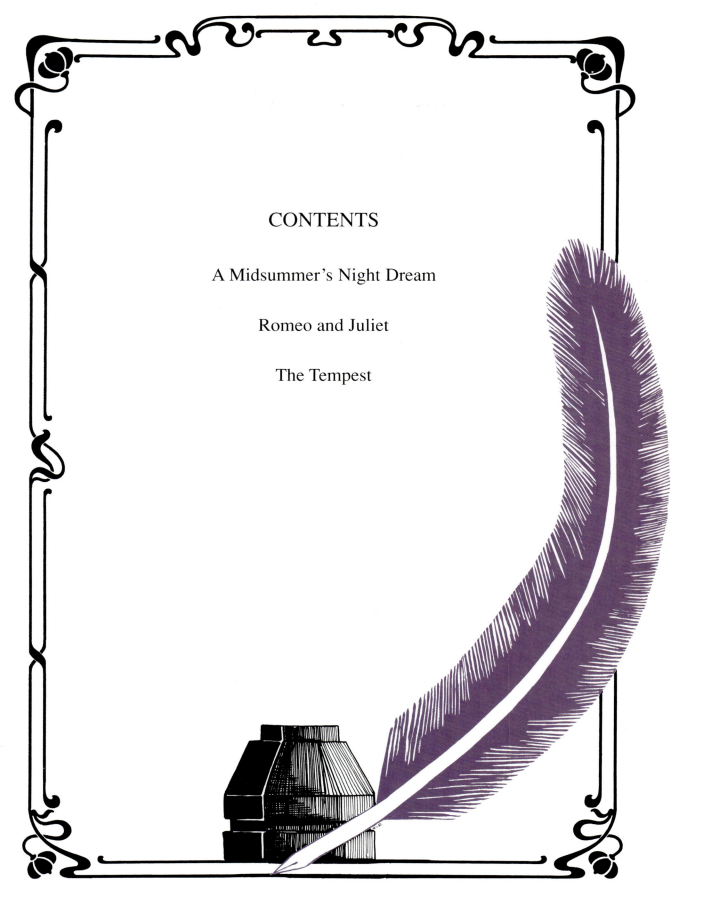

I would like to thank my family and friends
who entered the enchanted lands of imagination
to pose for the characters in this collection
of Shakespeare's tales.

CAST OF CHARACTERS

Stephanie A. Haasz-Morell — Titania
Joseph Tracy — Oberon
Timothy Tracy — Puck
Sharon Hind-Smith — Hermia
Patrick Hind-Smith — Lysander
Kathy Nichols — Helena
Steven Nichols — Demetrius
Bruce Grotta — Theseus
Walter Wood — Egeus
Jarritt Andre Logan — Indian Prince
Fairies and Elves:
Jill Grotta, Iris Kitagawa, Emily Ries Jacoby,
Walt Wood, April Wood, Betsy Dougherty, Brett Dougherty,
Trevor Nichols, Harold B. Hairston Jr.
Danielle Capriotti — Juliet
John D. Haasz — Romeo
Joseph Casale — Friar Lawrence
Warren Dikeman — Tybalt, Lord Paris, Benvolio
Jill Grotta — Lady Capulet
Michael Mastrangelo — Lord Capulet
Helen Mastrangelo — Lady Montegue
Harold Mastrangelo — Lord Montegue
Marcel Lambrecht — Mercutio
Charles Parsons — Prince
Guests at the ball:
Vered Hyman, Jochanan Hyman,
Sandy Wood, Walter Wood, Danny McLaughlin
Kimberly McCartney — Miranda
Joseph P. Henigan — Ferdinand; Prospero's brother; Calaban
Michael Mastrangelo — Prospero
Dante Zappala — Ariel
Jochanan Hyman — Gonzalo
Jerry Hyman — King of Naples

LIST OF ILLUSTRATIONS

A MIDSUMMER NIGHT'S DREAM

here was a law in the city of Athens, which gave to its citizens the power of compelling their daughters to marry whomsoever they pleased. Upon a daughter's refusing to marry a man her father had chosen to be her husband, the father was empowered by this law to cause her to be put to death. But as fathers do not often desire the death of their own daughters, even though they do happen to prove a little obstinate, this law was seldom or never put into execution, though perhaps the young ladies of that city were not unfrequently threatened by their parents with the terrors of it.

There was one instance, however, of an old man, whose name was Egeus, who actually did come before Theseus (at that time the reigning Duke of Athens) to complain that his daughter Hermia, whom he had commanded to marry Demetrius, a young man of noble Athenian family, refused to obey him, because she loved another young Athenian, named Lysander. Egeus demanded justice of Theseus, and desired that this cruel law might be put in force against his daughter.

Hermia pleaded in excuse for her disobedience that Demetrius had formerly professed love for her dear friend Helena, and that Helena loved Demetrius to distraction. However, this honorable reason which Hermia gave for not obeying her father's command moved not the stern Egeus.

Theseus, though a great and merciful prince, had no power to alter the laws of his country. He could only give Hermia four days to consider of it, and at the end of that time, if she still refused to marry Demetrius, she was to be put to death.

When Hermia was dismissed from the presence of the duke, she went to her lover, Lysander, and told him the peril she was in, and that she must either give him up and marry Demetrius, or lose her life in four days.

Lysander was in great affliction at hearing these evil tidings; but recollecting that he had an aunt who lived at some distance from Athens, and that at the place where she lived the cruel law could not be put in force against Hermia (this law not extending beyond the boundaries of the city), he proposed to Hermia that she should steal out of her father's house that night, and go with him to his aunt's house, where he would marry her. "I will meet you," said Lysander, "in the wood where we have so often walked with Helena in the pleasant month of May."

To this proposal Hermia joyfully agreed. She told no one of her intended flight but her friend Helena. Helena (as maidens will do foolish things for love) very ungenerously resolved to go and tell this to Demetrius. She could hope no benefit from betraying her friend's secret but the poor pleasure of following her faithless lover to the wood; for she well knew that Demetrius would go thither in pursuit of Hermia.

The wood, in which Lysander and Hermia proposed to meet, was the favorite haunt of those little beings known by the name of *Fairies*.

Oberon the king, and Titania the queen, of the fairies, with all their tiny train of followers, in this wood held their midnight revels.

Between this little king and queen of sprites there happened, at this time, a sad disagreement. They never met by moonlight in the shady walks of this pleasant wood but they were quarrelling, till all their fairy elves would creep into acorn-cups and hide themselves for fear.

The cause of this unhappy disagreement was Titania's refusing to give Oberon a little changeling boy, whose mother had been Titania's friend; and upon her death the fairy queen stole the child from its nurse, and brought him up in the woods.

The night upon which the lovers were to meet in this wood, as Titania was walking with some of her maids-of-honor, she met Oberon attended by his train of fairy courtiers.

"Ill met by moonlight, proud Titania," said the fairy king. The queen replied, "What! jealous Oberon, is it you? Fairies, skip hence; I have forsworn his company!" "Tarry, rash fairy!" said Oberon: "am not I thy lord? Why does Titania cross her Oberon? Give me your little changeling boy to be my page."

"Set your heart at rest," answered the queen; "your whole fairy kingdom buys not the boy of me." She then left her lord in great anger. "Well, go your way," said Oberon; "before the morning dawns I will torment you for this injury." Oberon then sent for Puck, his chief favorite and privy councillor.

Puck (or, as he was sometimes called, Robin Goodfellow) was a shrewd and knavish sprite, that used to play comical pranks in the neighboring villages. He was sometimes getting into the dairies and skimming the milk, sometimes plunging his light and airy form into the butter-churn, and while he was dancing his fantastic shape in the churn, in vain the dairymaid would labor to change her cream into butter. The village swains fared no better; whenever Puck chose to play his freaks in the brewing copper, the ale was sure to be spoiled. When a few good neighbours were met to drink some comfortable ale together, Puck would jump into the bowl of ale in the likeliness of a roasted crab, and when some old goody was going to drink

he would bob against her lips, and spill the ale over her withered chin. Presently after, when the same old dame was gravely seating herself to tell her neighbors a sad and melancholy story, Puck would slip her three-legged stool from under her, and down toppled the poor old woman, and then the old gossips would hold their sides and laugh at her, and swear they never wasted a merrier hour.

"Come hither, Puck," said Oberon to this little merry wanderer of the night. "Fetch me the flower which maids call 'Love in Idleness'; the juice of that little purple flower laid on the eyelids of those who sleep will make them, when they awake, dote on the first thing they see. Some of the juice of that flower I will drop on the eyelids of my Titania when she is asleep, and the first thing she looks upon when she opens her eyes she will fall in love with, even though it be a lion, or a bear, a meddling monkey, or a busy ape. And before I will take this charm from off her sight, which I can do with another charm know of, I will make her give me that boy to be my page."

Puck, who loved mischief to his heart, was highly diverted with this intended frolic of his master, and ran to seek the flower; and while Oberon was waiting the return of Puck, he observed Demetrius and Helena enter the wood. He overheard Demetrius reproaching Helena for following him, and after many unkind words on his part, and gentle expostulations from Helena, reminding him of his former love and professions of true faith to her, he left her (as he said) to the mercy of the wild beasts, and she ran after him as swiftly as she could.

The fairy king, who was always friendly to true lovers, felt great compassion for Helena, and perhaps, as Lysander said they used to walk by moonlight in this pleasant wood, Oberon might have seen Helena in those happy times when she was beloved by Demetrius. However that might be, when Puck returned with the little purple flower, Oberon said to his favorite, "Take a part of this flower: there has been a sweet Athenian lady here who is in love with a disdainful youth; if you find him sleeping, drop some of the love-juice in his eyes, but contrive to do it when she is near him, that the first thing he sees when he awakes may be this despised lady. You will know the man by the Athenian garments which he wears." Puck promised to manage this matter very dextrously, and then Oberon went, unperceived by Titania, to her bower, where she was preparing to go to rest. Her fairy bower was a bank, where grew wild thyme, cowslips, and sweet violets, under a canopy of woodbine, musk-roses, and eglantine. There Titania always slept some part of the night; her coverlet the enamelled skin of a snake, which, though a small mantle, was wide enough to wrap a fairy in.

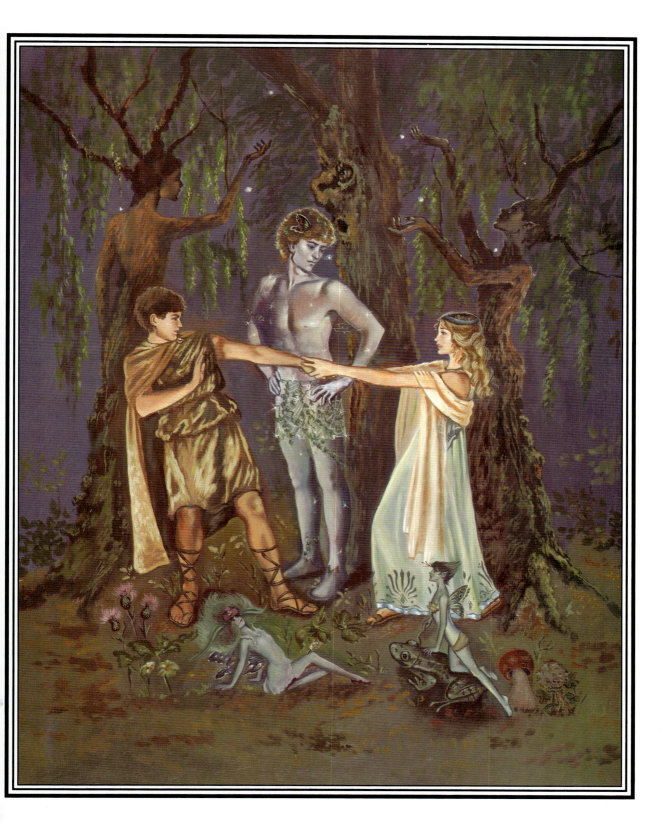

He found Titania giving orders to her fairies how they were to employ themselves while she slept. "Some of you," said her majesty, "must kill cankers in the musk-rose buds, and some wage war with the bats for their leathern wings to make my small elves coats, and some of you keep watch that the clamorous owl, that nightly hoots, come not near me; but first sing me to sleep." Then they began to sing this song:

> *"You spotted snakes with double tongue,*
> *Thorny hedgehogs, be not seen;*
> *Newts and blind-worms, do no wrong,*
> *Come not near our fairy queen.*
> *Philomel, with melody,*
> *Sing in your sweet lullaby,*
> *Lulla, lulla, lullaby; lulla, lulla, lullaby:*
> *Never harm, nor spell, nor charm,*
> *Come our lovely lady nigh;*
> *So good night with lullaby."*

When their fairies had sung their queen asleep with this pretty lullaby, they left her, to perform the important services she had enjoined them. Oberon then softly drew near his Titania, and dropped some of the love-juice on her eyelids, saying:

> *"What thou seest when thou dost wake,*
> *Do it for thy true-love take."*

But to return to Hermia, who made her escape out of her father's house that night to avoid the death she was doomed to for refusing to marry Demetrius. When she entered the wood she found her dear Lysander waiting for her, to conduct her to his aunt's house. Before they had passed half through the wood Hermia was so much fatigued that Lysander, who was very careful of this dear lady, who had proved her affection for him even by hazarding her life for his sake, persuaded her to rest till morning on a bank of soft moss. Then lying down himself on the ground at some little distance, they soon fell fast asleep. Here they were found by Puck, who, seeing a handsome young man asleep, and perceiving that his clothes were made in the Athenian fashion, and that a pretty lady was sleeping near him, concluded that this must be the Athenian maid and her disdainful lover whom Oberon had set him to seek. He naturally enough conjectured that, as they were alone together, she must be the first thing he would see when he awoke, so without more ado he proceeded to pour some of the juice of the little purple flower into his eyes. But it so fell out that Helena came that way, and, instead of Hermia, was the first object Lysander beheld when he opened his eyes; and, strange to relate, so powerful was the love-charm that all his love for Hermia vanished away, and Lysander fell in love with Helena.

Had he first seen Hermia when he awoke, the blunder Puck committed would have been of no consequence, for he could not love that faithful lady too well. But for poor Lysander to be forced by a fairy love-charm to forget his own true Hermia, and to run after another lady and leave Hermia asleep quite alone in a wood at midnight, was a sad chance indeed.

Thus this misfortune happened. Helena, as has been before related, endeavored to keep pace with Demetrius when he ran away so rudely from her, but she could not continue this unequal race long, men being always better runners in a long race than ladies. Helena soon lost sight of Demetrius, and as she was wandering about, dejected and forlorn, she arrived at the place where Lysander was sleeping. "Ah!" said she, "this is Lysander lying on the ground: is he dead or asleep?" Then gently touching him, she said, "Good sir, if you are alive, awake." Upon this Lysander opened his eyes, and (the love-charm beginning to work) immediately addressed her in terms of extravagant love and admiration. He told her she as much excelled Hermia in beauty as a dove does a raven, and that he would run through fire for her sweet sake, and many more such lover-like speeches. Helena, knowing Lysander was her friend Hermia's lover, and that he was solemnly engaged to marry her, was in the utmost rage when she heard herself addressed in this manner, for she thought (as well she might) that Lysander was making jest of her. "Oh!" said she, "why was I born to be mocked and scorned by everyone? Is it not enough, is it not enough, young man, that I can never get a sweet look or a kind word from Demetrius, but you, sir, must pretend in this disdainful manner to court me? I thought, Lysander, you were a lord of more true gentleness." Saying these words in great anger, she ran away, and Lysander followed her, quite forgetful of his own Hermia, who was still asleep.

When Hermia awoke, she was in a sad fright at finding herself alone. She wandered about the wood, not knowing what was become of Lysander, or which way to go to seek for him.

In the meantime Demetrius, not being able to find Hermia and his rival Lysander, and fatigued with his fruitless search, was observed by Oberon fast asleep. Oberon had learnt by some questions he had asked of Puck that he had applied the love-charm to the wrong person's eyes, and now having found the person first intended, he touched the eyelids of the sleeping Demetrius with the love-juice. He instantly awoke, and the first thing he saw being Helena, he, as Lysander had done before, began to address love speeches to her. Just at that moment Lysander, followed by Hermia (for through Puck's unlucky mistake it was

now become Hermia's turn to run after her lover), made his appearance, and then Lysander and Demetrius, both speaking together, made love to Helena, they being each one under the influence of the same potent charm.

The astonished Helena thought that Demetrius, Lysander, and her once dear friend Hermia were all in a plot together to make jest of her.

Hermia was as much surprised as Helena: she knew not why Lysander and Demetrius, who both before loved her, were now become the lovers of Helena, and to Hermia the matter seemed to be no jest.

The ladies, who before had always been the dearest of friends, now fell to high words together.

"Unkind Hermia," said Helena, "it is you have set Lysander on to vex me with mock praises; and your other lover Demetrius, who used almost to spurn me with his foot, have you not bid him call me goddess, nymph, rare, precious, and celestial? He would not speak thus to me, whom he hates, if you did not set him on to make a jest of me. Unkind Hermia to join with men in scorning your poor friend. Have you forgot our school-day friendship? How often, Hermia, have we two, sitting on one cushion, both singing one song, with our needles working the same flower, both on the same sampler wrought, growing up together in fashion of a double cherry, scarcely seeming parted? Hermia, it is not friendly in you, it is not maidenly, to join with men in scorning your poor friend."

"I am amazed at your passionate words," said Hermia: "I scorn you not; it seems you scorn me." "Ay, do!" returned Helena, "persevere, counterfeit serious looks, and make mouths at me when I turn my back; then wink at each other, and hold the sweet jest up. If you had any pity, grace, or manners, you would not use me thus."

While Helena and Hermia were speaking these angry words to each other, Demetrius and Lysander left them, to fight together in the wood for the love of Helena.

When they found the gentlemen had left them, they departed, and once more wandered weary in the wood in search of their lovers.

As soon as they were gone, the fairy king, who with little Puck had been listening to their quarrels, said to him, "This is your negligence, Puck; or did you do this wilfully?" "Believe me, king of shadows," answered Puck, "it was a mistake; did not you tell me I should know the man by his Athenian garments? However, I am not sorry this has happened, for I think their jangling makes excellent sport." "You heard," said Oberon, "that Demetrius and Lysander are gone to seek a convenient

place to fight in. I command you to overhang the night with a thick fog, and lead these quarrelsome lovers so astray in the dark that they shall not be able to find each other. Counterfeit each of their voices to the other, and with bitter taunts provoke them to follow you, while they think it is their rival's tongue they hear. See you do this till they are so weary they can go no farther, and when you find they are asleep, drop the juice of this other flower into Lysander's eyes, and when he awakes he will forget his new love for Helena, and return to his old passion for Hermia. Then the two fair ladies may each one be happy with the man she loves, and they will think all that has passed a vexatious dream. About this quickly, Puck, and I will go and see what sweet love my Titania has found."

Titania was still sleeping, and Oberon, seeing a clown near her who had lost his way in the wood, and was likewise asleep:—"This fellow," said he, "shall be my Titania's true-love"; and clapping an ass's head over the clown's, it seemed to fit him as well as if it had grown upon his own shoulders. Although Oberon fixed the ass's head on very gently, it awakened him, and rising up, unconscious of what Oberon had done to him, he went towards the bower where the fairy queen slept.

"Ah! what angel is that I see?" said Titania, opening her eyes, and the juice of the little purple flower beginning to take effect. "Are you as wise as you are beautiful?"

"Why, mistress," said the foolish clown, "if I have wit enough to find the way out of this wood, I have enough to serve my turn."

"Out of the wood do not desire to go," said the enamored queen. "I am a spirit of no common rate. I love you. Go with me, and I will give you fairies to attend upon you." She then called four of her fairies: their names were Pease-blossom, Cobweb, Moth, and Mustard-seed.

"Attend," said the queen, "upon this sweet gentleman; hop in his walks, and gambol in his sight; feed him with grapes and apricots, and steal for him the honey-bags from the bees. Come, sit with me," said she to the clown, "and let me play with your amiable hairy cheeks, my beautiful ass! and kiss your fair large ears, my gentle joy!"

"Where is Pease-blossom?" said the ass-headed clown, not much regarding the fairy queen's courtship, but very proud of his new attendants.

"Here, sir," said little Pease-blossom.

"Scratch my head," said the clown. "Where is Cobweb?"

"Here, sir," said Cobweb.

"Good Mr. Cobweb," said the foolish clown, "kill me the red humble-bee on

the top of that thistle yonder; and, good Mr. Cobweb, bring me the honey-bag. Do not fret yourself too much in the action, Mr. Cobweb, and take care the honey-bag break not; I should be sorry to have you overflown with a honey-bag. Where is Mustard-seed?"

"Here, sir," said Mustard-seed. "What is your will?"

"Nothing," said the clown, "good Mr. Mustard-seed, but to help Mr. Pease-blossom to scratch. I must go to a barber's, Mr. Mustard-seed, for methinks I am marvellous hairy about the face."

"My sweet love," said the queen, "what will you have to eat? I have a venturous fairy shall seek the squirrel's hoard, and fetch you some new nuts."

"I had rather have a handful of dried pease," said the clown, who with his ass's head had got an ass's appetite; "but, I pray, let none of your people disturb me, for I have a mind to sleep."

"Sleep, then," said the queen, "and I will wind you in my arms. O how I love you! How I dote upon you!"

When the fairy king saw the clown sleeping in the arms of his queen, he advanced within her sight, and reproached her with having lavished her favors upon an ass.

This she could not deny, as the clown was then sleeping within her arms, with his ass's head crowned by her flowers.

When Oberon had teased her for some time, he again demanded the changeling boy, which she, ashamed of being discovered by her lord with her new favorite, did not dare to refuse him.

Oberon, having thus obtained the little boy he had so long wished for to be his page, took pity on the disgraceful situation into which, by his merry contrivance, he had brought his Titania. He threw some of the juice of the other flower into her eyes; and the fairy queen immediately recovered her senses; and wondered at her late dotage, saying how she now loathed the sight of the strange monster. Oberon likewise took the ass's head from off the clown, and left him to finish his nap with his own fool's head upon his shoulders.

Oberon and his Titania being now perfectly reconciled, he related to her the history of the lovers, and their midnight quarrels. She agreed to go with him and see the end of their adventures.

The fairy king and queen found the lovers and their fair ladies, at not great distance from each other, sleeping on a grass-plot; for Puck, to make amends for his former mistake, had contrived with the utmost diligence to bring them all to the

same spot unknown to each other. He had carefully removed the charm from off the eyes of Lysander with the antidote the fairy king gave to him.

Hermia first awoke, and finding her lost Lysander asleep so near her, was looking at him and wondered at his strange inconstancy. Lysander presently opening his eyes, and seeing his dear Hermia, recovered his reason which the fairy charm had before clouded, and with his reason his love for Hermia. They began to talk over the adventures of the night, doubting if these things had really happened, or if they had both been dreaming the same bewildering dream.

Helena and Demetrius were by this time awake, and a sweet sleep having quieted Helena's disturbed and angry spirits, she listened with delight to the professions of love which Demetrius still made to her, and which, to her surprise as well as pleasure, she began to perceive were sincere.

These fair night-wandering ladies, now no longer rivals, became once more true friends. All the unkind words which had passed were forgiven and they calmly consulted together what was best to be done in their present situation. It was soon agreed that, as Demetrius had given up his pretension to Hermia, he should endeavor to prevail upon her father to revoke the cruel sentence of death which had been passed against her. Demetrius was preparing to return to Athens for this friendly purpose, when they were surprised with the sight of Egeus, Hermia's father, who came to the wood in pursuit of his runaway daughter.

When Egeus understood that Demetrius would not now marry his daughter, he no longer opposed her marriage with Lysander, but gave his consent that they should be wedded on the fourth day from that time, being the same day on which Hermia had been condemned to lose her life. On that same day Helena joyfully agreed to marry her loved and now faithful Demetrius.

The fairy king and queen, who were invisible spectators of this reconciliation, and now saw the happy ending of the lovers' history brought about through the good offices of Oberon, received so much pleasure that these kind spirits resolved to celebrate the approaching nuptials with sports and revels throughout their fairy kingdom.

And now, if any are offended with this story of fairies and their pranks, as judging it incredible and strange, they have only to think that they have been asleep and dreaming, and that all these adventures were visions which they saw in their sleep: and I hope none of my readers will be so unreasonable as to be offended with a pretty harmless Midsummer Night's Dream.

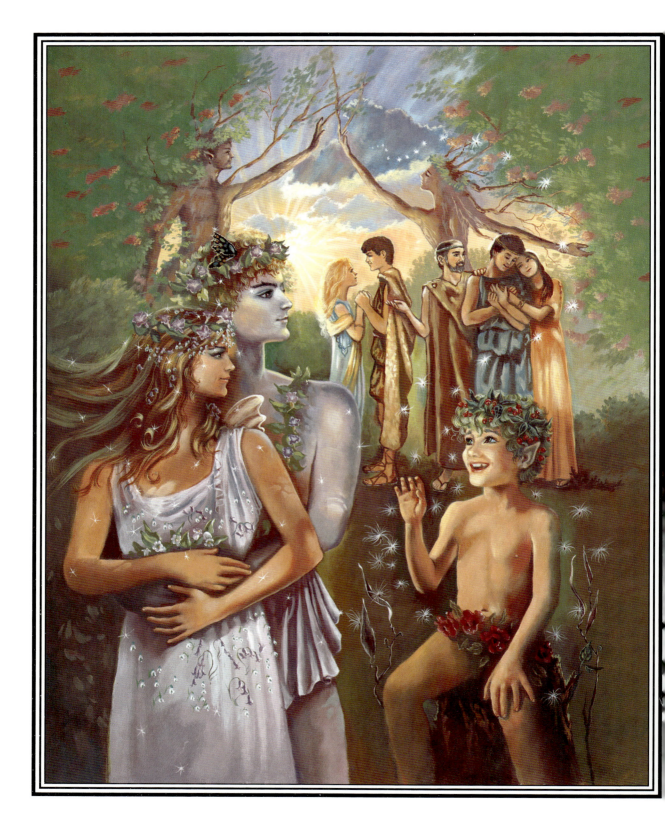

ROMEO AND JULIET

he two chief families in Verona were the rich Capulets and the Montagues. There had been an old quarrel between these families, which was grown to such a height, and so deadly was the hatred between them, that it extended to the remotest kindred, even to the followers and retainers of both sides. Insomuch that a servant of the house of Montague could not meet a servant of the house of Capulet, nor a Capulet encounter with a Montague by chance, but fierce words and sometimes bloodshed ensued. Frequent brawls from such accidental meetings disturbed the happy quiet of Verona's streets.

Old Lord Capulet made a great supper, to which many fair ladies and many noble guests were invited. All the admired beauties of Verona were present, and all comers were made welcome if they were not of the house of Montague. At this feast of the Capulets, Rosaline, beloved of Romeo, son to the old Lord Montague, was present. Though it was dangerous for a Montague to be seen in this assembly, Benvolio, a friend of Romeo, persuaded the young lord to go in this disguise of a mask that he might see his Rosaline, and seeing her, compare her with some choice beauties of Verona, who, he said, would make him think his swan a crow. Romeo had small faith in Benvolio's words; nevertheless, for the love of Rosaline, he was persuaded to go. Romeo was a sincere and passionate lover, and one that lost his sleep for love, and fled society to be alone thinking on Rosaline, who disdained him and never requited his love with the least show of courtesy or affection. Benvolio wished to cure his friend of this love by showing him the diversity of ladies and company. To this feast of the Capulets, then, young Romeo, with Benvolio and their friend Mercutio, went masked. Old Capulet bid them welcome, and told them that ladies who had their toes unplagued with corns would dance with them. The old man was light-hearted and merry, and said that he had worn a mask when he was young, and could have told a whispering tale in a fair lady's ear. And as they fell to dancing, Romeo was suddenly struck by the exceeding beauty of a lady who danced there. She seemed to him to teach the torches to burn bright, and her beauty to show by night like a rich jewel worn by a blackamoor. A beauty too rich for use, too dear for earth; like a snowy dove trooping with crows, he said, so richly did her beauty and perfections shine above her companions. While he uttered these praises he was overheard by Tybalt, a nephew of Lord Capulet, who knew him by his voice to be

Romeo. And this Tybalt, being of a fiery and passionate temper, could not endure that a Montague should come under cover of a mask to fleer and scorn, as he said, at their proceedings. He stormed and raged exceedingly, and would have struck young Romeo dead, but his uncle, the Lord Capulet, would not suffer him to do any injury at that time both out of respect to his guests and because Romeo had borne himself like a gentleman; which all tongues in Verona bragged of him to be a virtuous and well-governed youth. Tybalt, thus forced to be patient against his will, restrained himself, but swore that this vile Montague should at another time dearly pay for his intrusion.

The dancing being done, Romeo watched the place where the lady stood, and under favor of his masking habit, which might seem to excuse in part the liberty, he presumed in the gentlest manner to take her by her hand, calling it a shrine, which if he profaned by touching it, he was a blushing pilgrim and would kiss it for atonement. "Good pilgrim," answered the lady, "your devotion shows by far too mannerly and too courtly; saints have hands, which pilgrims may touch but kiss not." "Have not saints lips, and pilgrims too?" said Romeo. "Ay," said the lady, "lips which they must use in prayer." "Oh, then, my dear saint," said Romeo, "hear my prayer, and grant it lest I despair!" In such like allusions and loving conceits they were engaged when the lady was called away to her mother. Romeo, inquiring who her mother was, discovered that the lady whose peerless beauty he was so much struck with was young Juliet, daughter and heir to the Lord Capulet, the great enemy of the Montagues, and that he had unknowingly engaged his heart to his foe. This troubled him, but it could not dissuade him from loving.

As little rest had Juliet when she found that the gentleman that she had been talking with was Romeo and a Montague, for she had been suddenly smit with the same hasty passion for Romeo which he had conceived for her. A prodigious birth of love it seemed to her, that she must love her enemy, and that her affections should settle there where family considerations should induce her chiefly to hate.

It being midnight, Romeo with his companions departed; but they soon missed him, for unable to stay away from the house where he had left his heart, he leaped the wall of an orchard which was at the back of Juliet's house. Here he had not been long, ruminating on his new love, when Juliet appeared above at a window, through which her exceeding beauty seemed to break like the light of the sun in the east. The moon, which shone in the orchard with a faint light, appeared to Romeo as if sick and pale with grief at the superior luster of this new sun. And she leaning her hand upon her cheek, he passionately wished himself a glove upon that hand, that he

might touch her cheek. She all this while thinking herself alone, fetched a deep sigh, and exclaimed, "Ah me!"

Romeo, enraptured to hear her speak, said softly and unheard by her, "Oh, speak again, bright angel, for such you appear, being over my head like a winged messenger from heaven, whom mortals fall back to gaze upon!" She, unconscious of being overheard, and full of the passion which that night's adventure had given birth to, called upon her lover by name, whom she supposed absent, "O Romeo, Romeo!" said she, "wherefore art thou, Romeo? Deny thy father and refuse thy name for my sake; or if thou wilt not, be but my sworn love, and I no longer will be a Capulet." Romeo, having this encouragement, would fain have spoken, but he was desirous of hearing more. The lady continued her passionate discourse with herself, as she thought, still chiding Romeo for being Romeo and a Montague, and wishing him some other name, or that he would put away that hated name, and for that name, which was no part of himself, he should take all herself. At this loving word Romeo could no longer refrain, but taking up the dialogue as if her words had been addressed to him personally, and not merely in fancy, he bade her call him Love or by whatever other name she pleased, for he was no longer Romeo if that name was displeasing to her.

Juliet, alarmed to hear a man's voice in the garden, did not at first know who it was that, by favor of the night and darkness, had thus stumbled upon the discovery of her secret. But when he spoke again, though her ears had not yet drunk a hundred words of that tongue's uttering, yet so nice is a lover's hearing that she immediately knew him to be young Romeo. She rebuked him for the danger to which he had exposed himself by climbing the orchard walls, for if any of her kinsmen should find him there, it would be death to him, being a Montague. "Alack!" said Romeo, "there is more peril in your eye than in twenty of their swords. Do you but look kind upon me, lady, and I am proof against their enmity. Better my life should be ended by their hate, than that hated life should be prolonged to live without your love." "How came you into this place," said Juliet, "and by whose direction?" "Love directed me," answered Romeo. "I am no pilot, yet wert thou as far apart from me as that vast shore which is washed with the farthest sea, I should adventure for such merchandise." A crimson blush came over Juliet's face, yet unseen by Romeo by reason of the night, when she reflected upon the discovery she had made, yet not meaning to make it, of her love to Romeo. She would fain have recalled her words, but that was impossible. Fain would she have stood upon form and have kept her lover at a distance, as the custom of discreet ladies is, to frown and be perverse, and give their

suitors harsh denials at first. They must stand off, and affect a coyness or indifference where they most love, that their lovers may not think them too lightly or too easily won—for the difficulty of attainment increases the value of the object.

But there was no room in her case for denials, or puttings off, or any of the customary arts of delay and protracted courtship. Romeo had heard from her own tongue, when she did not dream that he was near her, a confession of her love, So, with an honest frankness which the novelty of her situation excused, she confirmed the truth of what he had before heard. She addressed him by the name of *fair Montague* (love can sweeten a sour name), she begged him not to impute her easy yielding to levity, or an unworthy mind, but that he must lay the fault of it, if it were a fault, upon the accident of the night, which had so strangely discovered her thoughts. She added, that though her behavior to him might not be sufficiently prudent, measured by the custom of her sex, yet that she would prove more true than many whose prudence was dissembling, and their modesty artificial cunning.

Romeo was beginning to call the heavens to witness that nothing was farther from his thoughts than to impute a shadow of dishonor to such an honored lady, when she stopped him, begging him not to swear, for although she joyed in him, yet she had no joy of that night's contract, for it was too rash, too unadvised, too sudden. But he being urgent with her to exchange a vow of love with him that night, she said that she already had given him hers before he requested it, meaning when he overheard her confession, but she would retract what she then bestowed, for the pleasure of giving it again, for her bounty was as infinite as the sea, and her love as deep. From this loving conference she was called away by her nurse, who slept with her, and thought it time for her to be in bed, for it was near to daybreak. Hastily returning, she said three or four words more to Romeo, the purpose of which was, that if his love was indeed honorable, and his purpose marriage, she would send a messenger to him tomorrow, to appoint a time for their marriage. Then she would lay all her fortunes at his feet, and follow him as her lord through the world. While they were settling this point, Juliet was repeatedly called for by her nurse, and went in and returned, and went and returned again, for she seemed as jealous of Romeo going from her as a young girl of her bird, which she will let hop a little from her hand, and pluck it back with a silken thread. Romeo was as loth to part as she, for the sweetest music to lovers is the sound of each other's tongues at night. But at last they parted, wishing mutually sweet sleep and rest for that night.

The day was breaking when they parted, and Romeo, who was too full of thoughts of his mistress and that blessed meeting to allow him to sleep, instead of

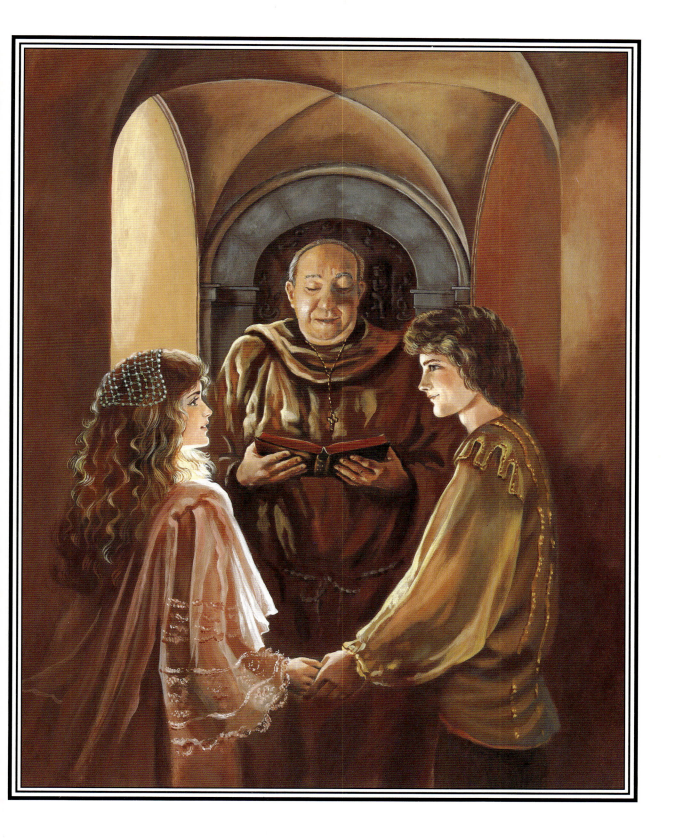

going home, bent his course to a monastery hard by, to find Friar Lawrence. The good friar was already up at his devotions, but seeing young Romeo abroad so early, he conjectured rightly that he had not been abed that night, but that some distemper of affection had kept him waking. He was right in imputing the cause of Romeo's wakefulness to love, but he made a wrong guess at the object, for he thought that his love for Rosaline had kept him waking. But when Romeo revealed his new passion for Juliet, and requested the assistance of the friar to marry them that day, the holy man lifted up his eyes and hands in a sort of wonder at the sudden change in Romeo's affections. He had been privy to all Romeo's love for Rosaline, and his many complaints of her disdain, and he said that young men's love lay not truly in their hearts, but in their eyes. But Romeo replying that he himself had often chided him for doting on Rosaline, who could not love him again, whereas Juliet both loved and was beloved by him, the friar assented in some measure to his reasons. A matrimonial alliance between young Juliet and Romeo might happily be the means of making up the long breach betweeen the Capulets and the Montagues, which no one more lamented than this good friar, who was a friend to both the families. Often he interceded to make up the quarrel without effect, partly moved by policy, and partly by his fondness for young Romeo, to whom he could deny nothing, the old man consented to join their hands in marriage.

Now was Romeo blessed indeed, and Juliet, who knew his intent from a messenger which she had despatched according to promise, did not fail to be early at the cell of Friar Lawrence, where their hands were joined in holy marriage. The good friar prayed to the heavens to smile upon that act, and in the union of this young Montague and young Capulet to bury the old strife and long dissensions of their families.

The ceremony being over, Juliet hastened home, where she stayed impatient for the coming of night, at which time Romeo promised to come and meet her in the orchard where they had met the night before. The time between seemed as tedious to her as the night before some great festival seems to an impatient child, that has got new finery which it may not put on till the morning.

That same day about noon, Romeo's friends, Benvolio and Mercutio, walking through the streets of Verona, were met by a party of the Capulets with the impetuous Tybalt at their head. This was the same angry Tybalt who would have fought with Romeo at old Lord Capulet's feast. He, seeing Mercutio, accused him bluntly of associating with Romeo, a Montague. Mercutio, who had as much fire and youthful blood in him as Tybalt, replied to this accusation with some sharpness.

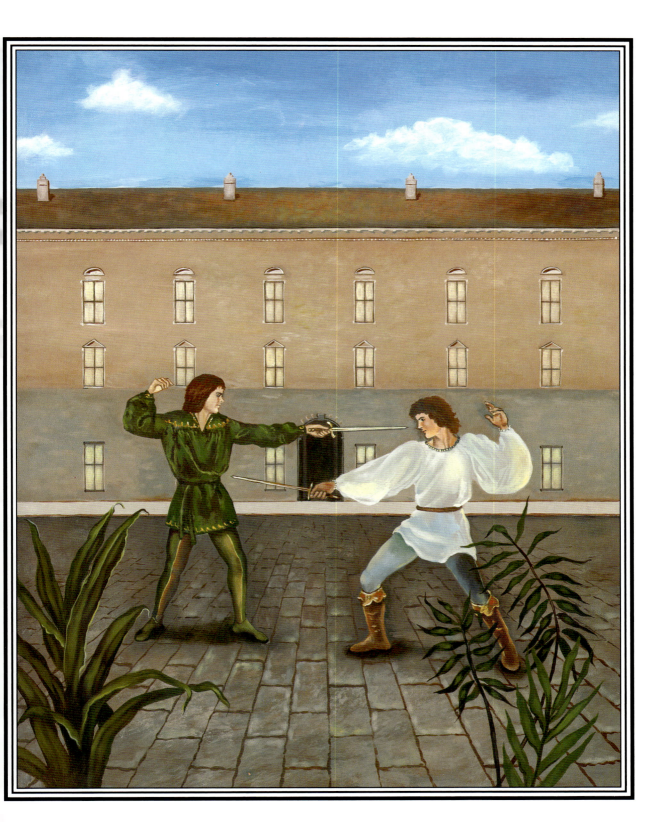

In spite of all Benvolio could say to moderate their wrath, a quarrel was beginning, when Romeo himself passing that way, the fierce Tybalt turned from Mercutio to Romeo, and gave him the disgraceful appellation of "villain."

Romeo wished to avoid a quarrel with Tybalt above all men, because he was the kinsman of Juliet, and much beloved by her. Besides, this young Montague had never thoroughly entered into the family quarrel, being by nature wise and gentle; and the name of a Capulet, which was his dear lady's name, was now rather a charm to allay resentment than a watchword to excite fury. So he tried to reason with Tybalt, whom he saluted mildly by the name of *good Capulet*, as if he, though a Montague, had some secret pleasure in uttering that name. But Tybalt, who hated all Montagues as he hated hell, would hear no reason. He drew his weapon, and Mercutio, who knew not of Romeo's secret motive for desiring peace with Tybalt, but looked upon his present forbearance as a sort of calm, dishonorable submission, with many disdainful words provoked Tybalt to the prosecution of his first quarrel with him. Tybalt and Mercutio fought till Mercutio fell, receiving his death's wound while Romeo and Benvolio were vainly endeavoring to part the combatants.

Mercutio being dead, Romeo kept his temper no longer, but returned the scornful appellation of "villain" which Tybalt had given him, and they fought till Tybalt was slain by Romeo. This deadly broil falling out in the midst of Verona at noonday, the news of it quickly brought a crowd of citizens to the spot, and among them the old Lords Capulet and Montague, with their wives. Soon after arrived the prince himself, who being related to Mercutio, whom Tybalt had slain, and having had the peace of his government often disturbed by these brawls of Montagues and Capulets, came determined to put the law in strictest force against those who should be found to be offenders. Benvolio, who had been eyewitness to the fray, was commanded by the prince to relate the origin of it, which he did, keeping as near to the truth as he could without injury to Romeo, softening and excusing the part which his friends took in it.

Lady Capulet, whose extreme grief for the loss of her kinsman Tybalt made her keep no bounds in her revenge, exhorted the prince to do strict justice upon his murderer, and to pay no attention to Benvolio's representation, who being Romeo's friend and a Montague, spoke partially. Thus she pleaded against her new son-in-law and Juliet's husband. On the other hand was to be seen Lady Montague pleading for her child's life, and arguing with some justice that Romeo had done nothing worthy of punishment in taking the life of Tybalt, which was already forfeited to the law by his having slain Mercutio. The prince, unmoved by the passionate exclama-

tions of these women, on a careful examination of the facts, pronounced his sentence and by that sentence Romeo was banished from Verona.

Heavy news to young Juliet, who had been but a few hours a bride, and now by this decree seemed everlastingly divorced! When the tidings reached her, she at first gave way to rage against Romeo, who had slain her dear cousin. She called him a beautiful tyrant, a fiend angelical, a ravenous dove, a lamb with a wolf's nature, a serpent heart hid with a flowering face, and other like contradictory names, which denoted the struggles in her mind between her love and her resentment. But, in the end, love got the mastery, and the tears which she shed for grief that Romeo had slain her cousin, turned to drops of joy that her husband lived whom Tybalt would have slain. Then came fresh tears, and they were altogether of grief for Romeo's banishment. That word was more terrible to her than the death of many Tybalts.

Romeo, after the fray, had taken refuge in Friar Lawrence's cell, where he was first made acquainted with the prince's sentence, which seemed to him far more terrible than death. To him it appeared there was no world out of Verona's walls, no living out of the sight of Juliet. Heaven was there where Juliet lived, and all beyond was purgatory, torture, hell. The good friar would have applied the consolation of philosophy to his griefs, but this frantic young man would hear of none. Like a madman he tore his hair, and threw himself all along upon the ground, as he said, to take the measure of his grave. From this unseemly state he was roused by a message from his dear lady, which revived him a little, whereas the friar took the advantage to rebuke him on the unmanly weakness which he had shown. He had slain Tybalt, but would he also slay himself, slay his dear lady who lived but in his life? The noble form of man, he said, was but a shape of wax, when it wanted the courage which should keep it firm. The law had been lenient to him, that, instead of death which he had incurred, had pronounced by the prince's mouth only banishment. He had slain Tybalt, but Tybalt would have slain him, there was a sort of happiness in that. Juliet was alive, and (beyond all hope) had become his dear wife, therein he was most happy. All these blessings, as the friar made them out to be, did Romeo put from him like a sullen misbehaved wench. And the friar bade him beware, for such as despaired (he said) died miserable. Then when Romeo was a little calmed, he counselled him that he should go that night and secretly take his leave of Juliet, and thence proceed straightway to Mantua, at which place he should stay till the friar found a fit occasion to publish his marriage. It might prove to be a joyful means of reconciling their families, and then he did not doubt but the prince would be moved to pardon him, and he would return with twenty times more joy than he went forth

with grief. Romeo was convinced by these wise counsels of the friar, and took his leave to go and seek his lady, purposing to stay with her that night, and by daybreak pursue his journey alone to Mantua. The good friar promised to send him letters from time to time, acquainting him with the state of affairs at home.

That night Romeo passed with his dear wife, gaining secret admission to her chamber from the orchard in which he had heard her confession of love the night before. That had been a night of unmixed joy and rapture. The pleasures of this night, and the delight which these lovers took in each other's society, were sadly allayed with the prospect of parting, and the fatal adventures of the past day. The unwelcome daybreak seemed to come too soon. When Juliet heard the morning song of the lark, she would fain have persuaded herself that it was the nightingale, which sings by the night, but it was too truly the lark which sang, and a discordant and unpleasing note it seemed to her, and the streaks of day in the east too certainly pointed out that it was time for these lovers to part. Romeo took his leave of his dear wife with a heavy heart, promising to write to her from Mantua every hour in the day. When he had descended from her chamber window, as he stood below her on the ground, in that sad foreboding state of mind in which she was, he appeared to her eyes as one dead in the bottom of a tomb. Romeo's mind misgave him in like manner, but now he was forced hastily to depart, for it was death for him to be found within the walls of Verona after daybreak.

This was but the beginning of the tragedy of this pair of star-crossed lovers. Romeo had not been gone many days before the old Lord Capulet proposed a match for Juliet. The husband he had chosen for her, not dreaming that she was married already, was Count Paris, a gallant, young, and noble gentleman, no unworthy suitor to the young Juliet, if she had never seen Romeo.

The terrified Juliet was in a sad perplexity at her father's offer. She pleaded her youth unsuitable to marriage, the recent death of Tybalt, which had left her spirits too weak to meet a husband with any face of joy, and how indecorous it would show the family of the Capulets to be celebrating a nuptial feast, when his funeral solemnities were hardly over. She pleaded every reason against the match but the true one, namely that she was married already. But Lord Capulet was deaf to all her excuses, and ordered her to get ready, for the following Thursday she should be married to Paris. Lord Capulet having found her a husband rich, young, and noble, such as the proudest maid in Verona might joyfully accept, he could not bear that out of an affected coyness, as he construed her denial, she should oppose obstacles to her own good fortune.

In this extremity Juliet applied to the friendly friar, always her counsellor in distress. The friar asked her if she had resolution to undertake a desperate remedy, and she answering that she would go into the grave alive rather than marry Paris, her own dear husband living; he directed her to go home, and appear merry, and give her consent to marry Paris, according to her father's desire. Then on the next night, which was the night before the marriage, to drink-off the contents of a phial which he then gave to her, the effect of which would be, that for two-and-forty hours after drinking it she should appear cold and lifeless. When the bridegroom came to fetch her in the morning, he would find her to appearance dead; that then she would be borne, as the manner in that country was, uncovered on a bier, to be buried in the family vault. If she could put off womanish fear, and consent to this terrible trial, in forty-two hours after swallowing the liquid (such was its certain operation) she would be sure to awake, as from a dream; and before she should awake, he would let her husband know their drift, and he should come in the night, and bear her thence to Mantua.

Love, and the dread of marrying Paris, gave young Juliet strength to undertake this horrible adventure. She took the phial of the friar, promising to observe his directions.

Going from the monastery, she met the young Count Paris, and, modestly dissembling, promised to become his bride. This was joyful news to the Lord Capulet and his wife. It seemed to put youth into the old man, and Juliet, who had displeased him exceedingly by her refusal of the count, was his darling again, now she promised to be obedient. All things in the house were in a bustle against the approaching nuptials. No cost was spared to prepare such festival rejoicings as Verona had never before witnessed.

On the Wednesday night Juliet drank off the potion. She had many misgivings, lest the friar, to avoid the blame which might be imputed to him for marrying her to Romeo, had given her poison; but then he was always known for a holy man; then lest she should awake before the time that Romeo was to come for her. Would the terror of the place, a vault full of dead Capulets' bones, and where Tybalt all bloody, lay festering in his shroud, not be enough to drive her distracted; again she thought of all the stories she had heard of spirits haunting the place where their bodies were bestowed. But then her love for Romeo, and her aversion for Paris, returned, and she desperately swallowed the draught, and became insensible.

When young Paris came early in the morning with music, to awaken his bride, instead of living Juliet, her chamber presented the dreary spectacle of a

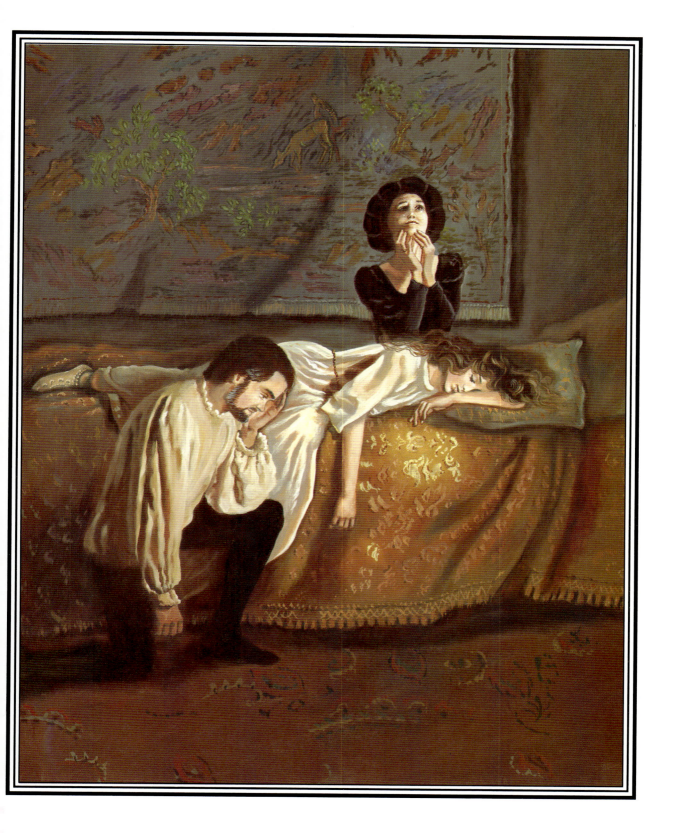

lifeless corpse. What death to his hopes! What confusion then reigned through the whole house! Poor Paris lamenting his bride, whom most detestable death had beguiled him of, had divorced from him even before their hands were joined. But still more piteous it was to hear the mournings of old Lord Capulet and Lady Capulet. They having but this one, one poor loving child, to rejoice and solace in, cruel death had snatched her from their sight, just as these careful parents were on the point of seeing her advanced (as they thought) by a promising and advantageous match. Now all things that were ordained for the festival were turned from their properties to do the office of a black funeral. The wedding cheer served for a sad burial feast, the bridal hymns were changed to sullen dirges, the sprightly instruments to melancholy bells, and the flowers that should have been strewed in the bride's path now served but to strew her corpse. Now, instead of a priest to marry her, a priest was needed to bury her; and she was borne to church indeed, not to augment the cheerful hopes of the living, but to swell the dreary numbers of the dead.

Bad news, which always travels faster than good, now brought the dismal story of his Juliet's death to Romeo at Mantua. The messenger had not yet arrived, who was sent from Friar Lawrence to apprise him that these were mock funerals only, and but the shadow and representation of death; and that his dear lady lay in the tomb but for a short while, expecting when Romeo should come to release her from that dreary mansion.

Just before, Romeo had been unusually joyful and light-hearted. He had dreamed in the night that he was dead (a strange dream, that gave a dead man leave to think), and that his lady came and found him dead, and breathed such life with kisses on his lips, that he revived, and was an emperor! And now that a messenger came from Verona, he thought surely it was to confirm some good news which his dreams had foretold. But when the contrary to this flattering vision appeared, and that it was his lady who was dead in truth, whom he could not revive by any kisses, he ordered horses to be got ready, for he determined that night to visit Verona, and to see his lady in her tomb. Mischief is swift to enter into the thoughts of desperate men. He called to mind a poor apothecary, whose shop in Mantua he had lately passed. From the beggarly appearance of the man, who seemed famished, and the wretched show in his shop of empty boxes ranged on dirty shelves and other tokens of extreme wretchedness, he had said at the time (perhaps having some misgivings that his own disastrous life might haply meet with a conclusion so desperate), "If a man were to need poison, which by the law of Mantua it is death to sell, here lives a

poor wretch who would sell it him." These words of his now came into his mind, and he sought out the apothecary, who, after some pretended scruples, Romeo offering him gold which his poverty could not resist, sold him a poison, which if he swallowed, he told him, if he had the strength of twenty men, would quickly despatch him.

With this poison he set out for Verona, to have a sight of his dear lady in her tomb, meaning, when he had satisfied his sight, to swallow the poison and be buried by her side. He reached Verona at midnight, and found the churchyard, in the midst of which was situated the ancient tomb of the Capulets. He had provided a lantern, and a spade, and a wrenching-iron, and was just proceeding to break open the monument, when he was interrupted by a voice, which, by the name of *vile Montague*, bade him desist from his unlawful business.

It was the young Count Paris, who had come to the tomb of Juliet at that un-seasonable time of night to strew flowers, and to weep over the grave of her that should have been his bride. He knew not what an interest Romeo had in the dead, but knowing him to be a Montague, and (as he supposed) a sworn foe to all the Capulets, he judged that he was come by the night to do some villainous shame to the dead bodies. In an angry tone he bade him desist; and, as a criminal, condemned by the laws of Verona to die if he were found within the walls of the city, he would have apprehended him.

Romeo urged Paris to leave him, and warned him by the fate of Tybalt, who lay buried there, not to provoke his anger, or draw down another sin upon his head, by forcing him to kill him. But the count in scorn refused his warning, and laid hands on him as a felon, which Romeo resisting, they fought, and Paris fell. Romeo, by the help of a light, came to see who is was that he had slain, and found it was Paris, who (he learned in his way from Mantua) should have married Juliet. He took the dead youth by the hand, as one whom misfortune had made a companion, and said that he would bury him in a triumphal grave, meaning in Juliet's grave. He opened the grave, and there lay his lady, as one whom death had no power upon to change a feature or complexion in her matchless beauty, or as if death were amorous, and the lean abhorred monster kept her there for his delight. She lay yet fresh and blooming, as she had fallen to sleep when she swallowed that benumbing potion, and near her lay Tybalt in his bloody shroud, whom Romeo seeing, begged pardon of his lifeless corpse, and for Juliet's sake called him *cousin*, and said that he was about to do him a favor by putting his enemy to death.

Here Romeo took his last leave of his lady's lips, kissing them, and then shed

the burden of his weary body by swallowing the poison which the apothecary had sold him, whose operation was fatal and real, not like that dissembling potion which Juliet had swallowed. The effect was now nearly expiring, and she about to awake to complain that Romeo had not kept his time, or that he had come too soon.

For now the hour was arrived at which the friar had promised that she should awake, and he, having learned that his letters, which he had sent to Mantua, by some unlucky detention of the messenger, had never reached Romeo, came now himself. Provided with a pickaxe and lantern, he sought to deliver the lady from her confinement, but he was surprised to find a light already burning in the Capulets' monument, and to see swords and blood near it, and Romeo and Paris lying breathless by the monument.

Before he could entertain a conjecture, to imagine how these fatal accidents had fallen out, Juliet awoke out of her trance. Seeing the friar near her, she remembered the place where she was, and the occasion of her being there, and asked for Romeo; but the friar, hearing a noise, bade her come out of that place of death and of unnatural sleep, for a greater Power than they could contradict had thwarted their intents. Being frighted by the noise of people coming, he fled, but when Juliet saw the cup closed in her true love's hands, she guessed that poison had been the cause of his end. She would have swallowed the dregs if any had been left, and she kissed his still warms lips to try if any poison yet did hang upon them, then hearing a nearer noise of people coming, she quickly unsheathed a dagger which she wore, and stabbing herself, died by her true Romeo's side.

The watch by this time had come up to the place. A page belonging to Count Paris, who had witnessed the fight between his master and Romeo, had given the alarm, which had spread among the citizens, who went up and down the streets of Verona confusedly exclaiming, "A Paris! a Romeo! a Juliet!" as the rumor had imperfectly reached them. The uproar brought Lord Montague and Lord Capulet out of their beds, with the prince, to inquire into the causes of the disturbance. The friar had been apprehended by some of the watch, coming from the churchyard, trembling, sighing, and weeping in a suspicious manner. A great multitude being assembled at the Capulets' monument, the friar was demanded by the prince to deliver what he knew of these strange and disastrous accidents.

And there, in the presence of the old Lords Montague and Capulet, he faithfully related the story of their children's fatal love, the part he took in promoting their marriage in the hope that the union would end the long quarrels between their families. How Romeo, there dead, was husband to Juliet, and Juliet, there dead, was

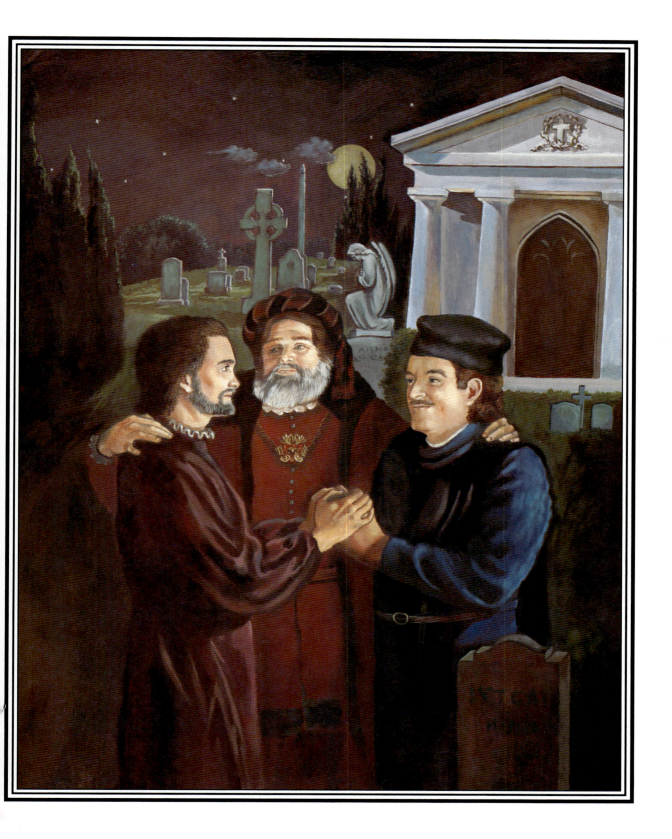

Romeo's faithful wife. How before he could find a fit opportunity to divulge their marriage, another match was projected for Juliet, who, to avoid the crime of a second marriage, swallowed the sleeping draught (as he advised), and all thought her dead. How, meantime, he wrote to Romeo, to come and take her thence when the force of the potion should cease, and by what unfortunate miscarriage of the messenger the letters never reached Romeo. Further than this the friar could not follow the story, nor knew more than that, coming himself to deliver Juliet from that place of death, he found the Count Paris and Romeo slain.

The remainder of the explanation was supplied by the narration of the page, who had seen Paris and Romeo fight, and by the servant who came with Romeo from Verona, to whom this faithful lover had given letters to be delivered to his father in the event of his death. They made good the friar's words, confessing his marriage with Juliet, imploring the forgiveness of his parents, acknowledging the buying of the poison of the poor apothecary, and his intent in coming to the monument, to die, and lie with Juliet. All these circumstances agreed together to clear the friar from any hand he could be supposed to have had in these complicated slaughters, further than as the unintended consequences of his own well-meant yet too artificial and subtle contrivances.

And the prince, turning to these old lords, Montague and Capulet, rebuked them for their brutal and irrational hatred, and showed them what a scourge Heaven had laid upon such offences, that it had found means even through the love of their children to punish their unnatural hate. These old rivals, no longer enemies, agreed to bury their long strife in their children's graves. Lord Capulet requested Lord Montague to give him his hand, calling him by the name of brother, as if in acknowledgment of the union of their families by the marriage of the young Capulet and Montague, and saying that Lord Montague's hand (in token of reconcilement) was all that he demanded for his daughter's jointure. But Lord Montague said he would give him more, for he would raise her statue of pure gold, that while Verona kept its name, no figure should be so esteemed for its richness and workmanship as that of the true and faithful Juliet. And Lord Capulet, in return, said that he would raise another statue to Romeo. So did these poor old lords, when it was too late, strive to outgo each other in mutual courtesies; while, so deadly had been their rage and hatred in past times, that nothing but the fearful overthrow of their children (poor sacrifices to their quarrels and dissensions!) could remove the rooted hates and jealousies of the noble families.

THE TEMPEST

here was a certain island in the sea, the only inhabitants of which were an old man, whose name was Prospero, and his daughter Miranda, a very beautiful young lady. She came to this island so young that she had no memory of having seen any other human face than her father's. They lived in a cave or cell, made out of a rock: it was divided into several apartments, one of which Prospero called his study. There he kept his books, which chiefly treated of magic, a study at that time much affected by all learned men, and the knowledge of this art he found very useful to him. For being thrown by a strange chance upon this island, which had been enchanted by a witch called Sycorax, who died there a short time before his arrival, Prospero, by virtue of this art, released many good spirits that Sycorax had imprisoned in the bodies of large trees. She did this because they had refused to execute her wicked commands. These gentle spirits were ever after obedient to the will of Prospero. Of these Ariel was the chief.

The lively little spirit Ariel had nothing mischievous in his nature, except that he took rather too much pleasure in tormenting an ugly monster called Caliban, for he owed him a grudge because he was the son of his old enemy Sycorax. This Caliban Prospero found in the woods, a strange misshapen thing, far less human in form than an ape. He took him home to his cell, and taught him to speak; and Prospero would have been very kind to him, but the bad nature which Caliban inherited from his mother Sycorax would not let him learn anything good or useful. Therefore, he was employed like a slave to fetch wood and do the most laborious offices, and Ariel had the charge of compelling him to these services.

When Caliban was lazy and neglected his work, Ariel (who was invisible to all eyes but Prospero's) would come slyly and pinch him, and sometimes tumble him down in the mire; and then Ariel, in the likeness of an ape, would make mouths at him. Then swiftly changing his shape, in the likeness of a hedgehog he would lie tumbling in Caliban's way, who feared the hedgehog's sharp quills would prick his bare feet. With a variety of such-like vexatious tricks Ariel would often torment him, whenever Caliban neglected the work which Prospero commanded him to do.

Having these powerful spirits obedient to his will, Prospero could by their means command the winds and the waves of the sea. By his orders they raised a violent storm, in the midst of which, and struggling with the wild sea-waves that every moment threatened to swallow it up, he showed his daughter a fine large ship, which he told her was full of living beings like themselves. "O my dear father," said she, "if by your art you have raised this dreadful storm, have pity on their sad distress. See! the vessel will be dashed to pieces. Poor souls! they will all perish. If I had power, I would sink the sea beneath the earth, rather than the good ship should be destroyed, with all the precious souls within her."

"Be not so amazed, daughter Miranda," said Prospero; "there is no harm done, I have so ordered it that no person in the ship shall receive any hurt. What I have done has been in care of you, my dear child. You are ignorant who you are, or where you came from, and you know no more of me but that I am your father, and live in this poor cave. Can you remember a time before you came to this cell? I think you cannot, for you were not then three years of age."

"Certainly I can, sir," replied Miranda.

"By what?" asked Prospero; "by any other house or person? Tell me what you can remember, my child."

Miranda said, "It seems to me like the recollection of a dream. But had I not once four or five women who attended upon me?"

Prospero answered, "You had, and more. How is it that this still lives in your mind? Do you remember how you came here?"

"No, sir," said Miranda, "I remember nothing more."

"Twelve years ago, Miranda," continued Prospero, "I was Duke of Milan, and you were a princess and my only heir. I had a younger brother, whose name was Antonio, to whom I trusted everything. As I was fond of retirement and deep study, I commonly left the management of my state affairs to your uncle, my false brother (for so indeed he proved). I, neglecting all worldly ends, buried among my books, did dedicate my whole time to the bettering of my mind. My brother Antonio, being this in possession of my power, began to think himself the duke indeed. The opportunity I have him of making himself popular among my subjects awakened in his bad nature a proud ambition to deprive me of my dukedom. He soon effected with the aid of the King of Naples, a powerful prince, who was my enemy."

"Wherefore," said Miranda, "did they not at that hour destroy us?"

"My child," answered her father, "they durst not, so dear was the love that my people bore me. Antonio carried us on board a ship, and when we were some leagues out at sea, he forced us into a small boat, without either a tackle, sail, or mast. There he left us, as he thought, to perish. But a kind lord of my court, one Gonzalo, who loved me, had privately placed in the boat water, provisions, apparel, and some books which I prize above my dukedom."

"O my father," said Miranda, "what a trouble must I have been to you then!"

"No, my love," said Prospero, "you were a little cherub that did preserve me. Your innocent smiles made me to bear up against my misfortunes. Our food lasted till we landed on this desert island, since when my chief delight has been in teaching you, Miranda, and well have you profited by my instructions."

"Heaven thank you, my dear father," said Miranda. "Now pray tell me, sir, your reason for raising this sea-storm?"

"Know, then," said her father, "that by means of this storm my enemies, the King of Naples and my cruel brother, are cast ashore upon this island."

Having so said, Prospero gently touched his daughter with his magic wand, and she fell fast alseep, for the spirit Ariel just then presented himself before his master, to give an account of the tempest, and how he had disposed of the ship's company. Though the spirits were always invisible to Miranda, Prospero did not choose she should hear him holding converse (as would seem to her) with the empty air.

"Well, my brave spirit," said Prospero to Ariel, "how have you performed your task?"

Ariel gave a lively description of the storm, and of the terrors of the mariners; and how the King's son, Ferdinand, was the first who leaped into the sea. His father thought he saw his dear son swallowed up by the waves and lost.

"But he is safe," said Ariel, "in a corner of the isle, sitting with his arms folded sadly, lamenting the loss of the King his father, whom he concludes drowned. Not a hair of his head is injured, and his princely garments, though drenched in the sea-waves, look fresher than before."

"That's my delicate Ariel," said Prospero. "Bring him hither: my daughter must see this young prince. Where is the King and my brother?"

"I left them," answered Ariel, "searching for Ferdinand, whom they have little hopes of finding, thinking they saw him perish. Of the ship's crew not one is missing, though each one thinks himself the only one saved. The ship, though invisible to them, is safe in the harbor."

"Ariel," said Prospero, "thy charge is faithfully performed; but there is more work yet."

"Is there more work?" said Ariel. "Let me remind you, master, you have promised me my liberty. I pray remember I have done you worthy service. I have told you no lies, made no mistakes, served you without grudge or grumbling."

"How now!" said Prospero. "You do not recollect what a torment I freed you

from. Have you forgot the wicked witch Sycorax, who with age and envy was almost bent double? Where was she born? Speak: tell me."

"Sir, in Algiers," said Ariel.

"O was she so?" said Prospero. "I must recount what you have been, which I find you do not remember. This bad witch Sycorax, for her withcrafts, too terrible to enter human hearing, was banished from Algiers, and here left by the sailors. Because you were a spirit too delicate to execute her wicked commands, she shut you up in a tree, where I found you howling. This torment, remember, I did free you from."

"Pardon me, dear master," said Ariel, ashamed to seem ungrateful; "I will obey your commands."

"Do so," said Prospero, "and I will set you free." He then gave orders what further he would have him do, and away went Ariel, first to where he had left Ferdinand, and found him still sitting on the grass in the same melancholy posture.

"O my young gentleman," said Ariel, when he saw him, "I will soon move you. You must be brought, I find, for the Lady Miranda to have a sight of your pretty person. Come, sir, follow me." He then began singing:

"Full fathom five thy father lies:
Of his bones are coral made;
Those are pearls that were his eyes:
Nothing of him that doth fade
But doth suffer a sea-change
Into something rich and strange.
Sea-nymphs hourly ring his knell:
Hark, now I hear them, ding-dong-bell."

This strange news of his lost father soon roused the prince from the stupid fit into which he had fallen. He followed in amazement the sound of Ariel's voice, till it led him to Prospero and Miranda, who were sitting under the shade of a large tree. Now, Miranda had never seen a man before, except her own father.

"Miranda," said Prospero, "tell me what you are looking at yonder."

"O father," said Miranda, in a strange surprise, "surely this is a spirit. Lord! how it looks about! Believe me, sir, it is a beautiful creature. Is it not a spirit?"

"No, girl," answered her father; "it eats, and sleeps, and has senses such as we have. This young man you see was in the ship. He is somewhat altered by grief, or you might call him a handsome person. He has lost his companions, and is wandering about to find them."

Miranda, who thought all men had grave faces and grey beards like her father, was delighted with the appearance of this beautiful young prince. Ferdinand

seeing such a lovely lady in this desert place, and from the strange sounds he had heard expecting nothing but wonders, thought he was upon an enchanted island, and that Miranda was the goddess of the place, and as such he began to address her.

She timidly answered, she was no goddess, but a simple maid, and was going to give an account of herself, when Prospero interrupted her. He was well pleased to find they admired each other, for he plainly perceived they had (as we say) fallen in love at first sight. To try Ferdinand's constancy, he resolved to throw some difficulties in their way: therefore advancing forward, he addressed the prince with a stern air, telling him he came to the island as a spy, to take it from him who was the lord of it. "Follow me," said he. "I will tie your neck and feet together. You shall drink seawater; shell-fish, withered roots, and husks of acorn shall be your food."

"No," said Ferdinand, "I will resist such entertainment, till I see a more powerful enemy." He drew his sword, but Prospero, waving his magic wand, fixed him to the spot where he stood, so that he had no power to move.

Miranda hung upon her father, saying, "Why are you so ungentle? Have pity, sir; I will be his surety. This is the second man I ever saw, and to me he seems a true one."

"Silence!" said her father; "one word more will make me chide you, girl. What, an advocate for an impostor? You think there are no more such fine men, having seen only him and Caliban. I tell you, foolish girl, most men as far excel this as he does Caliban." This he said to prove his daughter's constancy; and she replied, "My affections are most humble. I have no wish to see a goodlier man."

"Come on, young man," said Prospero to the prince; "you have no power to disobey me."

"I have not, indeed," answered Ferdinand; and not knowing that it was by magic he was deprived of all power of resistance, he was astonished to find himself so strangely compelled to follow Prospero. Looking back on Miranda as long as he could see her, he said, as he went after Prospero into the cave, "My spirits are all bound up, as if I were in a dream; but this man's threats, and the weakness which I feel, would seem light to me if from my prison I might once a day behold this fair maid."

Prospero kept Ferdinand not long confined within the cell. He soon brought out his prisoner; and set him a severe task to perform, taking care to let his daughter know the hard labor he had imposed on him. Then pretending to go into his study, he secretly watched them both.

Prospero had commanded Ferdinand to pile up some heavy logs of wood.

Kings' sons not being much used to laborious work, Miranda soon after found her lover almost dying with fatigue.

"Alas!" said she, "do not work so hard; my father is at his studies, he is safe for these three hours: pray rest yourself."

"O my dear lady," said Ferdinand, "I dare not. I must finish my task before I take my rest."

"If you will sit down," said Miranda, "I will carry your logs the while." But this Ferdinand would by no means agree to. Instead of a help Miranda became a hindrance, for they began a long conversation, so that the business of log-carrying went on very slowly.

Prospero, who had enjoined Ferdinand this task merely as a trial of his love, was not at his books as his daughter supposed, but was standing by them, invisible, to overhear what they say.

Ferdinand inquired her name, which she told him, saying it was against her father's express command she did so.

Prospero only smiled at this first instance of his daughter's disobedience, for having his magic art caused his daughter to fall in love so suddenly, he was not angry that she showed her love by forgetting to obey his commands. And he listened well pleased to a long speech of Ferdinand's, in which he professed to love her above all the ladies he ever saw.

In answer to his praises of her beauty, which he said exceeded all the women in the world, she replied, "I do not remember the face of any woman, nor have I seen any more men than you, my good friend, and my dear father. How features are abroad, I know not; but believe me, sir, I would not wish any companion in the world but you, nor can my imagination form any shape but yours that I could like. But, sir, I fear I talk to you too freely, and my father's precepts I forget."

At this Prospero smiled, and nodded his head, as much as to say, "This goes on exactly as I could wish; my girl will be Queen of Naples."

And then Ferdinand, in another fine long speech (for young princes speak in courtly phrases), told the innocent Miranda he was heir to the crown of Naples, and that she should be his queen.

"Ah, sir!" said she, "I am a fool to weep at what I am glad of. I will answer you in plain and holy innocence, I am your wife, if you will marry me."

Prospero prevented Ferdinand's thanks by appearing visible before them.

"Fear nothing, my child," said he; "I have overheard, and approve of all you have said. And, Ferdinand, if I have too severely used you, I will make you rich

amends, by giving you my daughter. All your vexations were but my trials of your love, and you have nobly stood the test. Then as my gift, which your true love has worthily purchased, take my daughter, and do not smile that I boast she is above all praise." He then, telling them that he had business which required his presence, desired they would sit down and talk together till he returned. This command Miranda seemed not all disposed to disobey.

When Prospero left them, he called his spirit Ariel, who quickly appeared before him, eager to relate what he had done with Prospero's brother and the King of Naples. Ariel said he had left them almost out of their senses with fear at the strange things he had caused them to see and hear. When fatigued with wandering about and famished for want of food, he had suddenly set before them a delicious banquet. Just as they were going to eat, he appeared visible before them in shape of a harpy, a voracious monster with wings, and the feast vanished away. Then, to their utter amazement, this seeming harpy spoke to them. He reminded them of their cruelty in driving Prospero from his dukedom, leaving him and his infant daughter to perish in the sea, saying that for this cause these terrors were suffered to afflict them.

The King of Naples and Antonio, the false brother, repented the injustice they had done to Prospero. Ariel told his master he was certain their penitence was sincere, and that he, though a spirit, could not but pity them.

"Then bring them hither, Ariel," said Prospero; "if you, who are but a spirit, feel for their distress, shall not I, who am a human being like themselves, have compassion on them? Bring them quickly, my dainty Ariel."

Ariel soon returned with the King, Antonio, and old Gonzalo in their train, who had followed him, wondering at the wild music he played in the air to draw them on to his master's presence. This Gonzalo was the same who had so kindly provided Prospero formerly with books and provisions, when his wicked brother left him, as he thought, to perish in a open boat in the sea.

Grief and terror had so stupefied their senses that they did not know Prospero. He first discovered himself to the good old Gonzalo, calling him the preserver of his life. It was then his brother and the King knew he was the injured Prospero.

Antonio, with tears and sad words of sorrow and true repentance, implored his brother's forgiveness. The King expressed his sincere remorse for having assisted Antonio to depose his brother. Prospero forgave them, and upon their engaging to restore his dukedom, he said to the King of Naples, "I have a gift in store for you too"; and opening a door, showed him his son Ferdinand playing at chess with Miranda.

Nothing could exceed the joy of the father and the son at this unexpected meeting, for they each thought the other drowned in the storm.

"O wonder!" said Miranda, "what noble creatures these are! It must surely be a brave world that has such people in it."

The King of Naples was almost as much astonished at the beauty and excellent graces of the young Miranda as his son had been.

"Who is this maid?" said he; "she seems the goddess that has parted us, and brought us thus together."

"No, sir," answered Ferdinand, smiling to find his father had fallen into the same mistake that he had done when he first saw Miranda; "she is a mortal, but by immortal Providence she is mine: I chose her when I could not ask you, my father, for your consent, not thinking you were alive. She is the daughter of this Prospero, who is the famous Duke of Milan, of whose remown I have heard so much, but never saw him till now: of him I have received a new life; he has made himself to me a second father, giving me this dear lady."

"Then I must be her father," said the King; "but, oh! how oddly will it sound that I must ask my child forgiveness."

"No more of that," said Prospero; "let us not remember our troubles past, since they so happily have ended." And then Prospero embraced his brother, and again assured him of his forgiveness. Prospero said that a wise, overruling Providence had permitted that he should be driven from his poor dukedom of Milan that his daughter might inherit the crown of Naples, for that by their meeting in this desert island it had happened that the King's son had loved Miranda.

These kind words which Prospero spoke, meaning to comfort his brother, so filled Antonio with shame and remorse that he wept and was unable to speak. The kind old Gonzalo wept to see this joyful reconciliation, and prayed for blessings on the young couple.

Prospero now told them that their ship was safe in the harbor, and the sailors all on board her, and that he and his daughter would accompany them home the next morning. "In the meantime," said he, "partake of such refreshments as my poor cave affords, and for your evening's entertainment I will relate the history of my life from my first landing in this desert island." He then called for Caliban to prepare some food and set the cave in order. The company were astonished at the uncouth form and savage appearance of this ugly monster, who (Prospero said) was the only attendant he had to wait upon him.

Before Prospero left the island he dismissed Ariel from his service, to the

great joy of that lively little spirit. Though he had been a faithful servant to his master, Ariel was always longing to enjoy his free liberty, to wander uncontrolled in the air, like a wild bird, under green trees, among pleasant fruits and sweet-smelling flowers.

"My quaint Ariel," said Prospero to the little sprite when he made him free, "I shall miss you; yet you shall have your freedom."

"Thank you, my dear master," said Ariel; "but give me leave to attend your ship home with prosperous gales, before you bid farewell to the assistance of your faithful spirit; and then, master, when I am free, how merrily I shall live!"

Here Ariel sang this pretty song:

"Where the bee sucks, there suck I;
In a cowslip's bell I lie:
There I couch when owls do cry.
On the bat's back I do fly
After summer merrily.
Merrily, merrily, shall I live now
Under the blossom that hangs on the bough."

Prospero then buried deep in the earth his magical books and wand, for he was resolved never more to make use of the magic art. And having thus overcome his enemies, and being reconciled to his brother and the King of Naples, nothing now remained to complete his happiness but to revisit his native land, to take possession of his dukedom, and to witness the happy nuptials of his daughter Miranda and Prince Ferdinand. The King said the marriage should be instantly celebrated with great splendor on their return to Naples. At which place, under the safe convoy of the spirit Ariel, they, after a pleasant voyage, soon arrived.

ABOUT THE ILLUSTRATOR

Judy Mastrangelo was born in Granite City, Illinois. As a young girl, Judy liked books very much and became interested in art. Inspired by artists such as Maxfield Parrish, Jesse Wilcox Smith, and the Pre-Raphaelites, Judy began painting in acrylics, concentrating on classical fantasy figures. She uses real people for her models. Often they are her friends and family.

Shakespeare is Judy's third book for The Unicorn Publishing House. She has also illustrated *Pollyanna* and *Antique Fairy Tales*. She has painted images for calendars, greeting cards, posters, and record album covers. In addition, Judy's work has been displayed in galleries across America and Europe. Now living in Pennsylvania with her husband Michael, Judy is looking forward to illustrating many more books for Unicorn Publishing.